Any resemblance to persons, living or dead, or semi-dead or semi-living,
between the characters or pets in this book, are fictitious and coincidental.
All events described in this book are parody and comedy and should not be
taken too seriously or you will have triple bypass and be stressed out.
This is Roger's and Esther's creation and came from their twisted and silly minds.
This is what happens when you take naps, dream and eat well. Plus having daughters
who act like they know better than everyone, doesn't hurt either.

First published in the United States of America by Esther Yang and Roger Ziegler
August 2012

ISBN: 978-0-9882312-0-7

First Printing, August 2012
Copyright © Esther Yang and Roger P. Ziegler 2012

Printed in the United States of America, not China or Mars.
Book Cover and Interior Design by Christine Van Bree

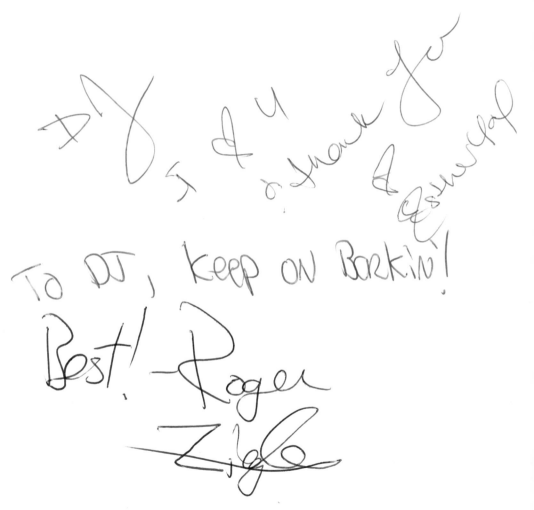

To DJ, keep on Barkin'!

Best! Roger

Ziglen

To Grace, Jaslyn, Abby and Chopstick,
the loves of our lives
and to Ellen Hauser for giving Abby to us.

Thank you to Kaicho Nakamura and all our Seido
karateka family for teaching us the "Sincere Way."

And gratitude to our parents and family for loving
us soooo much and driving us crazy at the same time
and hence providing the material for this book.

"Abby, the Superdog, appears to be a very wise canine indeed. Since we humans have to make do with two legs instead of four, I recommend reading Esther Yang and Roger Ziegler's new book of Abby's words of wisdom. As Abby says, "Happiness starts with you.""
DAVID LONGMIRE, PSYCHOTHERAPIST, NYC

"If you want to find inner peace, then this is the book for you."
CRAIG JONES, AUTHOR OF *FATAL ATTRACTION* AND *BLOOD SECRETS*

"This book is full of good life lessons for us all. Thanks, Abby!"
LYNN ALTMAN, PRESIDENT, BRAND NOW, AUTHOR OF *BRAND IT YOURSELF: THE FAST, FOCUSED WAY TO MARKETPLACE MAGIC*

"Esther's and Roger's book is a wonderful, realized idea. I have always thought that so much wisdom comes from our animals."
ANNIE BRADY, VISUAL ARTIST

"Funny with wise advice to a better life."
WESLEY E. BADILLO, MD, MPH, NYS DEPARTMENT OF HEALTH AIDS INSTITUTE

"I love this book. Dogs always let you know what they like. Wouldn't it be nice if all humans could be so honest."
CATHIE TUITE, DOG WALKER

"Forget this book, buy my book instead."
CHOPSTICK THE CAT, author of *THE BOOK OF SELF CONFIDENCE BY CHOPSTICK THE CAT*, a better sequel.

INTRODUCTION

Abby is the happiest, serene-iest, go-luckiest dog we know.
Except for thunder and the occasional small dog, nothing bothers her.
Not big mean dogs, not noisy vacuum cleaners, police sirens
or 5 am garbage trucks.

She is what Zen masters call, "super mellow."

We have distilled the essence of her teachings in this book.
You will discover how her blissful combination of quiet determination,
acceptance and calm allows her to deal with the most difficult situations.

We figure if it works for Abby and us, it will work for you.
So the next time you are facing an unreasonable boss or impossible relative;
Remember Abby and learn how to pee on it and walk away.

Take a nap. Learn to do this
with your eyes open and standing up.

Have a snack.
When your mouth is full,
you are less likely
to bite off someone's head.

Avoid **loud barking dogs**.
When you see or hear one, cross the street
and walk somewhere else until they
go away or stop barking.

Sniff out a friend and snuggle.
Sharing is caring.

Zip your lip and bite your tongue.
When you're tempted to fight, stop
and ask yourself, "Is this REALLY worth it?"

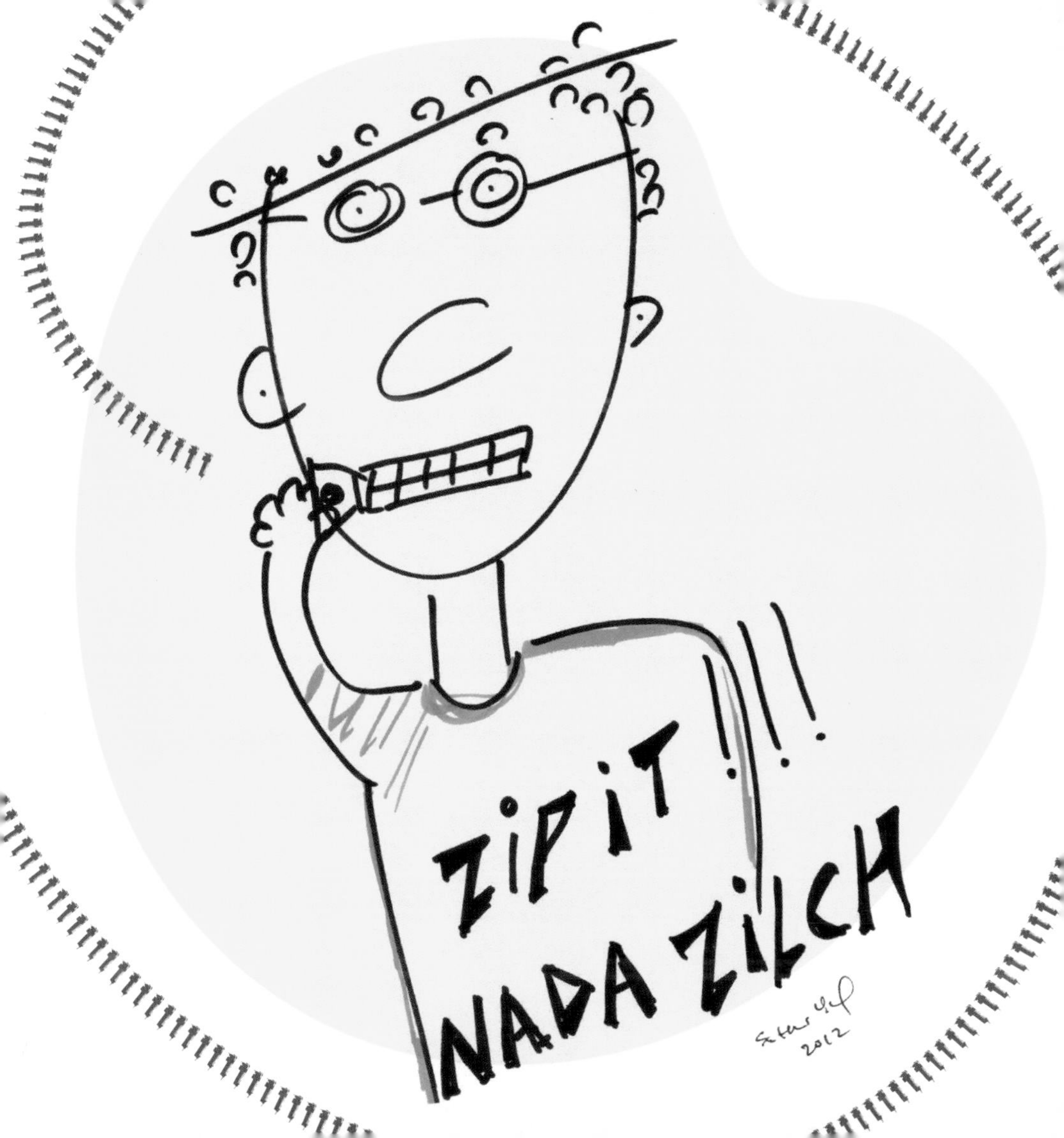
ZIP IT
NADA ZILCH
2012

Let *them* fetch.

Calm yourself by chanting, meditating, or doing a rain dance.

Life is short, think BIG.
Don't ever beg or settle for crumbs.

✵ ✵ ✵

Put *yourself* in "Time Out".

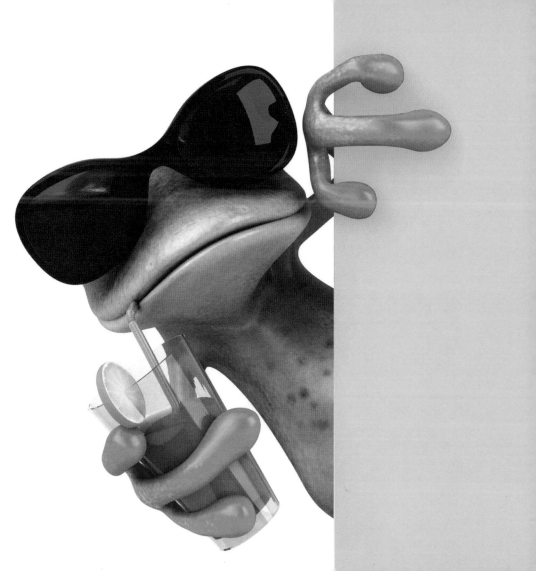

Be their #1 fan,
even if you want to vomit.

[If the room stinks, don't fart more.]

Hang out with bigger friends than you.

When you are the victim of a sneak attack,
ZOOM out of the way fast.

Write a sitcom
with all the free material
they are giving you.

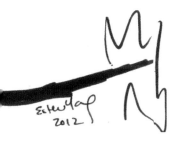

Angry dogs attract angry dogs.
Happy dogs attract everyone.
(except those who don't like dogs,
but you can't please everyone).

Make sure your own butt is clean first.

Their insanity is not *your* insanity.

Sweet voice, wag tail, widen eyes.

Be flexible. Do a cat pose.

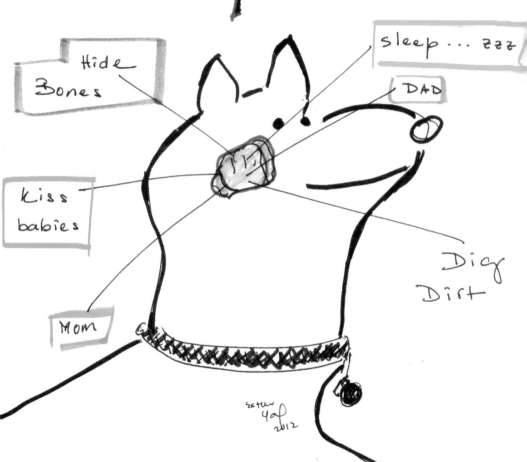

Don't let them live in your head rent free.

You can't fix stupid.
Don't even try.

Winning is not about being right.
It's about getting and keeping the pack together.

Comparing and despairing doesn't get you anywhere.

When someone criticizes you, or says, "bad dog!" they are really talking about themselves.

Don't get into a
pissing match with a skunk.
Others watching may not be able
to tell the difference.

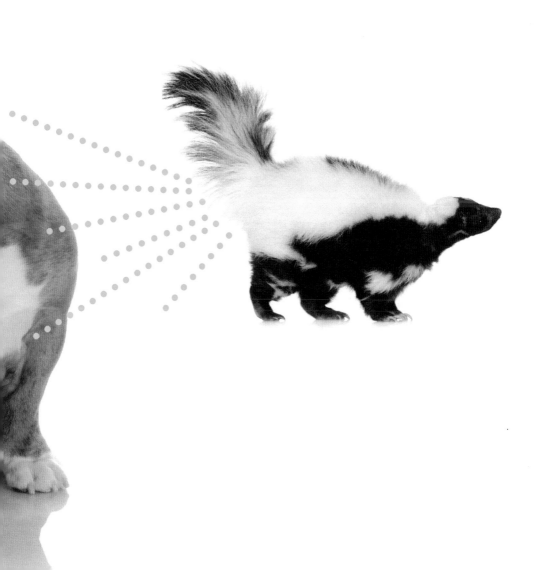

See them better than they see themselves.

Kindness and surrender are ultimately more powerful,
and effective, than anger.

If you pee on someone's leg,
say 'sorry' sincerely and clean it up.

Have a good hair day every day.

Say something nice.
A small compliment can defuse anger and
change someone's, and your, entire day.

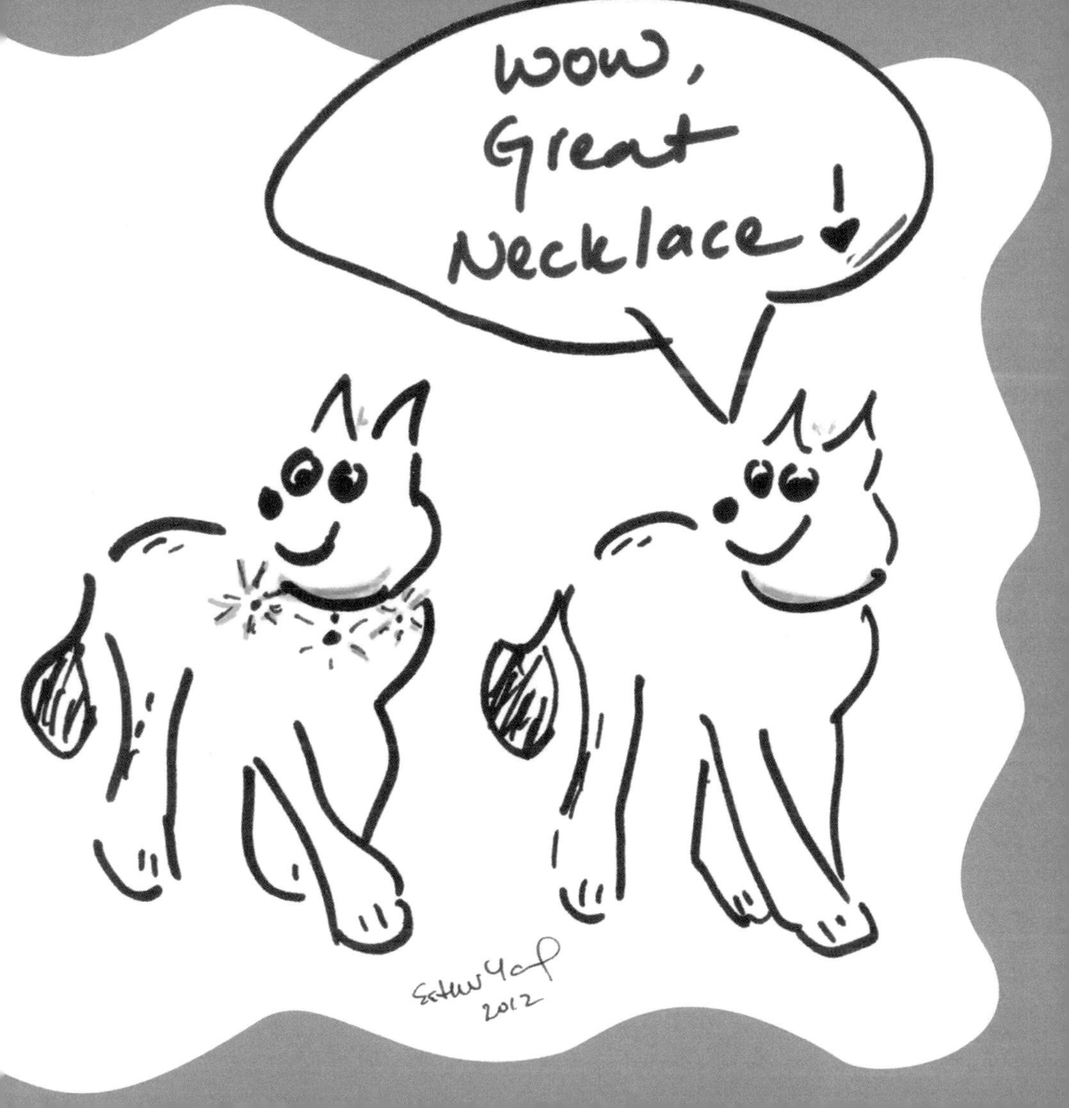
WOW, Great Necklace!

Happiness starts with you.

Don't be a difficult personality yourself.

• • •

If all else fails, lie (desperate times call for desperate measures).

Don't take it personally.
They are probably just hungry, angry, lonely or tired.

And remember,
the dog bowl is always full.

Hey. You. Forget the dog. Hunt down my, much better, sequel;
The Book of Self-Confidence by Chopstick the Cat:
How to get what you want and still be loved.
You'll learn my secrets for having it all, without the hairballs.

www.chopstickthecat.com

✷ ABOUT THE AUTHORS ✷

ABBY THE SUPERDOG is a 13 year old Chihuahua, Papillon and King Charles Spaniel mix. Abby lives in NYC with her sister, a calico cat named Chopstick, who loves to steal her food.

ESTHER YANG is a healer, Core Energetic Psychotherapist and Yoga teacher. She was born in Indonesia, studied in U.S. and Singapore. Esther is a graduate of Institute of Core Energetic and Barbara Brennan School of Healing. She has been featured on numerous television, radio programs and print publications. Esther often speaks about mind-body medicine to corporate and hospital groups, including Cornell Medical School, Learning Annex, Gilda's Club and Trinity Wall Street Discovery Ministry.

ROGER ZIEGLER is the author of several books for adults, young adults and children. An award-winning journalist and certified life coach, Roger has been featured in numerous publications and TV shows including NBC Nightly News, MBC  Korean Broadcasting, the *New York Times* and Australian *Cosmopolitan*. He hosts workshops where people unlock their powers for personal growth. His daughter Jaslyn is a wonderful artist.

Fetch more books at
www.peeandwalk.com

To book a speaking engagement contact:

Roger at roger@rogerziegler.com
or
Esther at esther@estheryang.com

Made in the USA
Charleston, SC
20 October 2012